Organchess

Peter Meinl-Kemper

the voidery aperture

First published in the United Kingdom in 2017
by
the Voidery Aperture

www.thevoideryaperture.com

All rights reserved

Copyright © Peter Meinl-Kemper, 2017

Peter Meinl-Kemper has asserted his right to be identified as author of this work in accordance with the Copyright, Designs and Patents Act, 1988.

This is a work of fiction. The names, characters, places, incidents and dialogues either are products of the author's imagination or are used fictitiously, and any resemblance to actual persons, living or dead, businesses, organizations, events or locales is entirely coincidental.

ISBN 978-0-9954812-2-0

*

they put you in charge of the man now he'd been born
how much like churches in the old days
solid Lucinda there   your case worker
a stirring of tendons and blood clots in the ruins
something to steer by
nipple-shaped runestones cupped in a palm
it hadn't been going too well for years
since he'd been born in fact
the fictions of his youth consigned to recycling bins
the imminent thing   the euphemist   in the ruins
a tearing of ligaments
and his case worker Lucinda
occasional truculence and the beadiness she aspired to
which she boasted of when she could
which was explained to you in passing
one of her rivals
either before or after the introductory briefing
need to recite inappropriate pieties
and sound as if you meant it
while they fucked you
how much like churches in the old days

*

there was a congregation   sort of
gossamer shock-victim foil of their capes
pinched round their shoulders as they knelt
glucosamine chalices at the ready
a body containing true believers and less-true ones
Lucinda wobbling along beside you
on her branded company hire-bike
veering off-message
old vulcanized bucket on secondment
being a toilet behind a screen
it was the restructuring to blame
it was the budgetary cuts
the impact of those swingeing cuts
on their business model
all to do with that

*

swabs at the door
your medical history
checks for allergy to latex
money well spent on that new striker
gloves snapped on
the slurp of lubricant
the smear with

Please use this space to help us capture any ideas you have for improving the range of services we provide
None   crossed that out
put something arch and supercilious
*I am constitutionally incapable of blue-sky thinking
horizon-gazing etc.*
supercilious but in a good way
poised   self-knowing
hint of a smirk about it   wry
*yeah but the transfer window's closing
our defence it's weak as water*
from the gusset some leisurely motes of dust dislodged
what essence of self   what shame to invest
best not to dwell   more questionnaire
you were an arse but you had righteousness on your side
dispensed   a mint for you to suck on while they probed
a plastic bowl between your legs
they took some photos

*

you were in charge of him
free agent that he was   was meant to be
he wasn't achieving
eyeball in close-up   expressive of terror

Lucinda   the liturgy   her obsession
breath like what's expelled from a five-year-old tyre
deflated in accordance with the manufacturer's
technical specifications
after a heavily laden trip round several countries
souls   repentance   these trainees
the body or congregation assuming a larger
share than before in the liturgy
and the liturgy more hardcore
better policed

*

leftover sandwiches for breakfast
late-night meetings overrun
cue jokes about doggy bags
cakes and pastries cheerfully mangled
in the comfort break succeeding Article 3
yeah free food's great
it's not like anyone actually pays
for stuff like sandwiches these days

Lucinda's breath   Lucinda's emphases
the housekeeping   fire regs   mutual expectations
earthworms halved in the sun-baked yard
a thrashing of red-jelly stumps
the rags of poisoned weeds
Lucinda's peaked cap that said *Pathway Lead*
her T-shirt saying *Helping You Achieve*

a migrant worker pushing the trolley round
how may I help you, sir
with compliments of the
have an outstanding weekend

*

only recall to yourself your debt which is our compact
in this vale of now-desalinated tears
the briefing   Lucinda
united in spirit if not in the letter of it
the care that underpins
she jolts you frowning from the shutters rolling down
your standing retreat
(yes that was her elbow)
need to recite inappropriate pieties
how the multitude recoils with a new facility
from compliance into compliance
benches crammed with avuncular knaves
the chatter of unsustainable slogans
crowdfunded orgiastic hope engulfing as hatred
time to loot ourselves
and everything we've worked for
keep this quiet   it's the antediluvian trove
that's what they're looting
only recall to yourself your debt
which is our compact

*

one of those oafs who get close up
and stay close up
however often you shuffle away protesting a virulent
cold or bacterial infection
straddling a branded company hire-bike
veering off-message
the bike and the T-shirt both too large for her
the trove and all its contents deleted by accident
how predictable
the scrambling for the reset button
the button that doesn't exist
Lucinda's theory that the trainees were repentant souls
in need of divine salvation
breathing heavily as she tried to regain control
and actually whimpering when she failed to
ploughing furrows in the decimated flowerbeds beyond
desalination of the tears perhaps an illusion
but that's how it seemed
how did she choose to define transgression
was all you asked
which brought her wobbling up alongside you
gasping doctrinal maxims angrily under her breath
you sensed the strengthening vacuous eloquence of the form
of that which is learned by rote and recited *in tenebris*
which through intimate long repetitions
gradually ceases to be just an adjunct to a theology
becoming instead a functional proxy for the theology
a process that might have provided a basis
for further discussion
if only you hadn't been with Lucinda
whom you slowed for
some kind of throbbing there in the cloaca
worms now halved into infinity

weeds resistant to every herbicide
known to the market
hire-bike wobbling on ahead

*

they didn't object while it was being done to them
they just lay there or kneeled there or hung there
went on squatting   stayed on all fours
generally dumb and unresponsive
like a corpse that hadn't gone stiff yet
but was rigid enough to hold the classic
pose you made it adopt
well not a great feat of imagination
when they'd put you in charge of the man
he wasn't achieving
tubes and cannulas and tubes
as though they were dogs in the fertile season
sniffing about
or people modelling outdoor clothing in a catalogue
nameless martyrs in the throes of blood-let rapture
plastic tables   plastic knives and forks and crockery
like they were chimpanzees
in a less-than-respectable zoo

*

tubes and catheters and lubricant
dressed according to someone's taste
and then undressed again
vest and pants
and rumours   talk of going too far
transgressing the boundaries of safety and good taste
apocryphal framework for complaints
that idle boasting in the shower-block
once I'm back in post, secure, I'll put such a fucking great fuck-off
negligence case together
just you wait
accreditation on watermarked paper
this was required
unique identifier   digitally captured signature
yeah cheeky fucking bastards won't know what's hit them
that was about as far as it went

*

Living Core Institutional Values in a World of Value Uncertainty
eminent reasonableness of the shirt
the sleeves rolled up   top button undone
the two breast pockets with fastened-down flaps
inviting confidence   at ease with keeping confidence
Please be advised that your facilitators today are Ruby and Jim
Ruby a no-show
Jim in his element   working the room
accreditation on watermarked paper
effortless   everything constantly opening up to the floor
with coffee and cake for inspiration   Jim called it *fika*
she preferred *breakout session*, Ruby did
and usually got her way
unique identifier   all good fun between colleagues
the *en suite* toilet
Jim said no-one needed to ask permission to use
a dusting of faecal particles
bran they resembled   or rolling tobacco
sprinkled on the moulded plastic seat
that they might actually be what they were
was oddly unthinkable
also a hair
what essence of self   what shame to invest
and someone called Ronnie who'd once shared a house
with five other people
six young bumholes   six busy owners of bumholes
one perfunctory rota   loosely observed
best not to dwell
I found I hated it slightly less if I could manage to convince myself that what I was brushing off with a wodge of toilet roll had come, you know, from a female bumhole, not like one of the guys'
Lucinda's stern interrogation
when she heard about it later

off-message again
inviolate sanctity of the confessional
not for Lucinda to plunder the safe space of the *fika*
and you hadn't been involved
you'd been introduced to them but didn't really know them
and you didn't want to join in
the peer disapproval
Ronnie's perception of the anus as a gendered thing
his tendency to sexualize what came out
it made him seem creepy
you think by cleaning mess off a toilet seat you were having some kind of sexual relationship with those girls?
poor Ronnie
he'd thought he could lighten the tone
instead he'd lowered it
really, this isn't at all in accordance with what I'd been led to believe was the latest in benchmarked good practice in this field
her delegate ID flipped the wrong way round on its ribbon
lodged in the folds of her polythene smock
besides, it wouldn't have been a woman who did that
leave stuff
women just don't

*

unknown visitors leaving tokens
of encouragement and esteem
sweet wrappers   lollipop sticks   a paperclip
your man, he could be famous
condoms (filled and knotted)
cracked biros
tea lights (spent)
you could be massive
riding his coat-tails, as they say
a wristwatch battery
pipe-cleaner stick-people
a tampon slightly clumped by incoming rain
just make him comfortable and viable again
he'll see you right
the latest restructuring developments
eight skilled operatives laid off
a gaping crenelated void left in the south-facing wall
where they'd downed tools that last day
Do Not Resuscitate
harping on   they said he was   always
nurse called Wilbur
when they took away his voice he ceased to sound like
where've they put the
nurse called Barbara
what I signed ngh
comedy robot
damp-course membrane
exposed at the base of the cutaway rhomboid
now a shelf for your accumulating perishables

*

next to you was drawing off rolls of dust
from where the dust lay unevenly fielded
tooling the rolls off into balls
and using these balls to form the basis of a structure
what he was doing was not at all crucial to the process
nor did it constitute an outcome
but it was keeping his mind off everything else in the room
I'm really excited by the prospect of getting to work with
lively engagement with the process
of embedding the rolling programme
of raising awareness
timely anecdote in the corner
not for general consumption
but actually highly pertinent
been let go for saying defilers of truth
who spray their shit over all that should be sacrosanct
been freed up so she can pursue new opportunities
exciting ones   elsewhere
I am, yes, totally committed to the project
clothed or naked
opened outwards or replete with unwashed inserts
maybe she hadn't explicitly called them defilers of truth
or made the accusation of spraying
but she'd been widely known to hold such views
her holding of them had shown
she'd been let go
and was assumed to be pursuing new opportunities
exciting ones   elsewhere
or being sprayed with liquid shit
the outcome couldn't be discounted
safe pair of hands
there was a pubic hair   stuck with saliva to the wall
there was a consensus on the question

of how to proceed
the structure was gradually revealed to be a pyramid
but there was insufficient dust in the local harvest
to complete it
real team player
pause to reflect on what's been junked
and you will fall behind
and possibly find yourself being sprayed with shit
the shit someone else's
building pipelines of talent   no silo mentality here
a schedule for downtime
from the process of embedment
as long as such downtime is to be used for the raising
of wider public awareness
regarding the rolling programme
of celebrating success
in the building of pipelines of talent
and breaking down silo mentalities
and not pausing to reflect on what has been junked
as this will mean falling behind
and possibly being sprayed with liquid shit
the shit someone else's
just like she had
new opportunities   exciting ones   elsewhere

*

a major step up for you they said
Lucinda's hard mentoring
to prove you're a serious person
ambient ionizing perfumes ordered in
to make the toilets smell a bit nicer
for the delegation of human-rights abusers
come to talk about investing in the brand
we've gained some real traction over this quartile
key esteem indicators continuing to accrue
your self-destructive attention to detail
consigned to recycling bins
an invoice gone unpaid
his situation   tubes   his catheter
hardly appropriate   you put in charge
I should be grateful if you'd confirm
a major step up for you
inhaling the latest superbugs through a clear straw
Dear Bill
I'm sorry to report that I've discovered an invoice dated
pumped up and down
and I will authorize emergency payment forthwith
Bill's ardent reply
dry mouth and panic   a scramble for guidelines
you have gone the extra mile in bringing this matter to our attention, I
am so sorry to tell you Hayley our valued colleague in accounts back
when none payment should have been flagged up and chased was
tragically assaulted leaving the premises late one evening dying two or
three weeks afterwards, to commemorate our dear colleague and say
thank you for your truly outstanding vigilance and care we'd like to
send you free of charge the brand new fragrance we created in her
memory naming it after her so your colleagues and yourself will maybe
think of her in your workplace from time to time
dry mouth and panic

Dear Bill
I'm very sorry to read
I'm sorry to hear
I do appreciate
unfortunately
I'm very much afraid
a rigorous framework in place
acceptance of corporate gifts

*

the wind fresh in from its cursory scouting-out
of brownfield investment opportunities
thirty metres over the threshold
tussling and fussing around the breezeblocks
further tokens of encouragement and esteem
on cratered ledges scurfy with peeling magnolia paint
small plastic pharmaceutical bottles
an invertebrate in each   poor scrabbling puny
questing mandibles
stoppered by smudged and twisted printouts
hi we'd like to be your friend
send debit card details and photo of rig
selectively rubberized
but uncovered in all the key places
employing a muscular golden-veined sex toy on herself
competitive rates, call now, no obligation quote
two tattooed buttocks stretched apart
extruding a pendant string of beads
join hardcore cavity fun, we're gagging to hear your voice!
huge standard-issue glabrous phallus
curved like a longbow in its engorgement
female nail extension   deep metallic crimson
probing the glans-cleft
Been fucked over? Sign up now
for instant hacks to fuck right back
a handwritten note lodged under a pumice stone
I should like to try again should you be willing

*

a thick coil of excrement   probably human
with some coins tamped in
the edge of each just visible
right, OK then guys, let's start and up the ante
Christ   the smell
*one for the gentlemen, the heterosexual gentlemen to begin with, though
I'm sure we'd welcome any and all contributions from any, ah, gay
friends or transgendered friends who might be present and have an
opinion to contribute*
on a plain white oval plate
*so, would it make the removal easier — not just more bearable, but
maybe even enjoyable or pleasurable — would it make the removal easier
if the poo had come from a female colleague's bottom instead of a
bloke's?*
had they rewarded hapless Ronnie with a strategic role
or input
*and if no takers still, how much would it take, on top of the basic value
of the coin itself, to persuade you to remove it?*
you'd never been good at batting it back
*and now we'll put that same set of questions to the ladies, heterosexual
ladies, present*
the well-meaning gesture instrumentalized by tyranny
will there be DNA or something?
can you tell the gender from that?
word gets round   you just aren't up to it
you're letting the whole team down
you're holding them back
from moving forward going forward
you know, I'd like to go back briefly to what
colleague over there
too fastidious about hygiene for your own good
scrubbing away like that   with not the softest tissue
in pursuit of some unattainable ideal

underpinning what you said, as I'm sure you're aware, is the same set of dodgy assumptions that underpin certain medieval notions of courtly love
after all   an arse is an arse
but who would claim that a pair of underpants
is anything more than an underpants?
nice-guy Jim   watch on the desk
the cavalry due with light refreshments
shall we comfort-break for ten first?
adjacent cubicle   gasping
whimpering at stool

*

you tried to articulate your grievances
not a complaint as such
quite clear where that would get you
(Lucinda's hard mentoring,
threat of an interview with the Human Capital Lead)
you *let off some steam*
just letting off steam
no more than that

*

thus profiting massively from the strategic
let it be branded
not a defence in the world could be conjured
happening everywhere only with infinite variety
in the aping of the massively
not a defence in the world to be uttered
not given to profiting   hiding or drifting
no defence in the world
but the wrong kind of stupefaction
you will be blacklisted for it   disgust
you couldn't speak out against it somehow
tried but somehow it undercut you
it outflanked you every time
if only you'd tried it
lacking the courage
but it was the context
it was context undercut you every time
and they owned the context
there could be nothing else but the context
every opposing gesture outflanked and obsolete
they'd made it their business to own the truth
or rather take ownership of the truth
so they could speak it
and many believed in it for up to a week at a time
or so you assumed
and thus profiting massively from it
they spoke

*

you tried to articulate your grievances
you failed

*

what Maisie called grounding
*take your shoes off, and your socks, if you're wearing socks — and yes,
the ladies, if you're wearing tights or stockings, slip them off too —
you'll see why soon — and once you're — you OK there, John? — so once
you're barefoot, in bare feet, we're looking to drop our awareness right
down into the soles of the feet, right where they touch the carpet*
elsewhere   some time other   before
*so what we're looking to do, right now, with all the focus of our
awareness on precisely this present moment — each present moment,
coming and going — what we're looking to do is feel each tiny
microscopic sensation of the skin against the carpet*
when this hadn't happened yet
when there was only a chance it would happen
a chance not a prospect
*don't get frustrated if you can't feel every fibre — that's not the object —
just letting the focus of our awareness sink to the soles of the feet and
stay there, being aware of any sensation that happens to come*
fallopian elegance of a motorway junction
uncoiling in the dawn
*and with each passing moment observing, without judging those
thoughts and sensations as they come — and just as importantly, trying
not to judge yourself or how well you're doing — that's not the object —
just observing whatever comes*
under the table: your daysack assisting in the deception
screening shod feet
that's any and all sensations and thoughts
dream of a long-dead dog restored to life
and bounding ahead of your motor scooter
the scooter itself ten years since rusted to death
*so now, if we're comfortable with that, if we could now each extend a
hand to touch the person on our left*
and then just taking a minute to register how that feels
a dolorous fart let slip at the back of the room

a snigger
you shouldn't expect to feel an 'energy flow' or anything fancy like that
we're just in the business of logging sensations here
just everyday sensations
are you OK with that, Marie-Claire?
not trying to judge ourselves, remember — just taking time to register
any and all sensations from that touch
a dutiful hand at your right elbow
fingernails nicotine yellow
engagement ring and wedding band
docking already in the cleft between your ribs and upper arm
so once you've spent a few moments registering those sensations, I'm
going to ask that next you move your hand, your left hand, to the chest
or groin of the person on your left
just staying relaxed now
moving slowly from wherever the hand is now — the elbow or shoulder —
to the area of the chest, or, if the moment says it's right, the general
area of the groin — the hand moving down or across, to cup the chest or
groin
settling gently   massaging gently
each participant staying open and receptive
staying alive to each and every sensation arising
waves of confusion and dismay
from the jumpered body to your left
self-pity or outrage
at the absence of physical contact
elsewhere   some time other   before
fallopian elegance of that motorway junction
something bizarrely like sympathy
for that sense of thwarted stakeholder compliance
somehow your touch
the long-dead dog restored to life
not lacking in influence   *soft power*
the power to make a body succumb
to what

itself   or something beyond itself
the long-dead dog still bounding on ahead
she had a name but it was painful to recall
not painful   sad
the hand with rings and yellow fingernails now delving
general region of your balls
worth getting away with
in the sense of throwaway   cheap
a cheeky memory for old age
hand paddling vaguely in mid-air
in lieu of seeking out and massaging
a gently jumpered nipple
some kind of throbbing there in the cloaca
thrashing of red-jelly stumps
the rags of poisoned weeds
a cramped sensation   no tumescence
fingernails   dirt   that opaque yellowing
you were shivering and it showed
if anyone needs to take a moment, that's perfectly fine
just gently lifting up the hand and disengaging, without judgement,
from the circle
blame those insects
those fried insects from the buffet
though you'd eaten none   eaten nothing
something like sympathy
for that sense of thwarted
stakeholder compliance

*

another discovery   in your sleep
you've been reduced to making noises like a pig
to think this could actually be happening to me
in public   noises like a pig
to think that this
his situation   tubes   his catheter
me reduced to
when they took away his voice he ceased to sound like
that this could be me
you made the discovery in your sleep
but you'd been making the porcine noises while awake
awake   and in public

*

pairing off to take their mindfulness practice further
being alive to each and every sensation that comes
reflections in bullet-point form
or as mind-maps
move on   find another partner
wipe-clean instructions
a bit like speed-dating
except we're not looking for speed, it's quite the opposite
be in the moment
one dribbling saliva into his partner's open mouth
then they swap round
one stroking the other's extruded tongue
in circular motions
applying the fingernail's ridge   the pad
the back of the fingernail   swap round
another pair taking turns to lick each other's eyeballs
another two studiously inhaling
from between each other's toes
change round   move on
insert a finger into a nostril
use your lips to clasp an earlobe
feint with a flickering motion   the tongue
bravura display of Nick's considerable skills
as a *people person*
Sadie affronted   glaring at shy-guy Todd
that's fifteen minutes of my life here
mindful gazing session gone wrong
that's fifteen minutes I won't get back
while doing her best to follow the broken
path of the breath down into her lungs
Todd trying hard also
even now   he won't even look at me
can you see why I'm finding this ever so slightly upsetting?

Todd signing up for the help
that would hone his skills
in maintaining appropriate eye contact
with colleagues
Sadie in turn persuaded to drop her planned complaint
against Todd on a charge of gross misconduct
pastries and sandwiches
then digital penetration of the anus
practised mindfully
Nick with the air of a man who knew
he was asking a lot
but who was confident he was capable
of delivering even more than he was asking
all it really is   it's just a leap of faith
it's really just trusting in yourselves as mindful practitioners
Vinnie and Lillian
smirking   dry-swallowing   up at the front
both visibly sick with trepidation
so now just popping your underwear down and bending over
Lillian turning back to face the group
and touching her throat and giggling
Vinnie frowning and coughing
and was he starting to cry?
and Nick nodding sagely
I think we'll leave that for the moment
wheeling an object on   an object under a dustsheet
what we'll do is, Vinnie and Lillian here, we'll show you how to apply
the lubricant safely, how to trim your nails and grease up so the exercise
is safe
and once you've done that, taken your turn, yeah? each with the
dummy, what we'll do is, then, we'll pair off so there's no-one too
exposed out at the front
and each pair of colleagues can find their own way
challenging exercise
be circulating

plenty of support
dustsheet whipped off
a life-size model of a person bending over
with a big effulgent anus
feeling better?
he was talking to you   this Nick was talking to you
I think you could really make a positive contribution to this exercise
if you'd like to pair up with Sadie here? no — Todd
pair up with Todd
your cratered ledges
scurfy with peeling magnolia paint
your sketched defence for the imminent hearing
with the Human Capital Lead

*

complications
what with everything being so tightly packed together
you haven't a hope of telling what's what
or where it is   it moves around   the source of the problem
you can't tell   one has to monitor all of this closely
it might be attributable to my habit
a stupid habit   I admit that
but defensible nevertheless   in a purely social sense
of holding in my farts all day when I must
and of being too strict in the muscularity of my clenching
or it might be I'm too brisk or even violent
in my wiping   too invasive
I've been fisting myself for years now, you could say
your sketched defence
unspoken   unsent

*

but what of the man
his situation wasn't improving
you were responsible for his care plan
pundits talking about that wish to die
that claim to wish to die
in the context of ethics
charge of the man now he'd been born
in charge of the man
when did that   when did you agree
the sort of sick that admits no prospect of recovery
wanting to die   no longer capable
of doing what needs to be done
he's left it too long
the eyeball in close-up   expressive of terror
pundits standing round   looking down at
in hushed voices
body enmeshed in its patchy chrysalis
of circuitry and tubes
the man seen staring
at a death that can't come soon enough
but is still months away
a year perhaps   or longer
at the wrong end of a sewer pipe of shame
and soundless screaming he's being dragged through
in a rivulet of his own faeces

*

place set for one in the basement bistro
folded newspaper   the daily bottle of red
the quiet *flâneur* you might have tried evolving into
absolute fantasy now
the worn and weary spinster
formerly strict now flaking morals
crossing the corridor
thankless comfort   once a week

*

don't let me get to that stage ever
if it seems I'm going to go that way just go ahead and shoot me
tip the pills in
straddle my guts and press down hard on my face with the pillow
the context of ethics
pundits by way of critique   their analysis
question of moral responsibility?
ramifications of a life extinguished in anger or despair?
the obligations that the dead lay on the living?
the would-be dead
you're holding them back from going forward

*

two daily bottles now
absolute fantasy
still kept neat
your single room
what thankless comfort
once a   what
what flaking morals
corridor   where

*

she's with a client
personal secretary to the Human Capital Lead
can you come back in twenty minutes?
he looks sad
should we refer him to the Counselling Team?
or Occupational Health?
new therapies   comforting sessions
a chance to roll around naked
in a pit of toothless puppies
Nick's new workshops   out of hours
Developing Mindful Anilingual Skills for Wellbeing
Maisie's claim that Nick had stolen her idea
and been promoted for the theft
her swift demotion
not a team player

*

Linnie can see you now
her office with its sunken bath full of puppies
cameras on tripods
screens suspended from the ceiling
so the issue here   portfolio of evidence
systematic noncompliance
one breast out   a puppy suckling
what exactly is the nature of your grievance
family photos on the desk
we're looking to reach out with a dialogue of mutual respect
ah   going forward
but what of the man
a rolling programme of mediation with collegiate
what of this man they
we could organize some help in the form of additional class-based
guidance on personal / interpersonal synergies
charged with the welfare of this man
might help to make you more of an integrated team player
in sessions like these
the pup tugging hard on the HCL's distended nipple
ah   certificate   ah   of exemption
situation wasn't improving
but you'll need to engage with the programme   rolling programme
class-based guidance
interpersonal   ah   synergies
going forward

*

new therapies   comforting sessions
the odd persistent notion
that you needed to be comforted
not tempted by the puppies?
self-disgust at your complicity
but you wanted that certificate
really popular those puppies
there's a waiting list
invitation to lie down
so   just relax now
nice lie-down
we're here to comfort you
the novelty of it   the strangeness
made your hand   allowed your hand
the long-dead dog restored to life
to rove around   to feel all sorts of
bounding ahead   your motor scooter
nape of her neck
the crease of her armpit opened a crack
the uppermost breast slumped over the lower one
then the midriff
which was soft and also slumped
and then the curve of the topmost hip
surprise of the mound
surprise of some pubic hairs on a mound
you didn't get pubic hairs on a mound
as much as you used to
she gave a gasp
she yanked your hand aside quite firmly
rusted to death
what are you doing?
partly a hiss and partly a whisper
there was no-one else in the therapy suite

Get Naked Suite
no clothes on
she'd just wanted to give you a hug

*

    pace of change   last quartile
    up but not sufficient
    must generate further traction   change
    transformative action
    from the steering group   attendance desired
    compulsory?   desired   but in your interest
    Innovation Lead's impassioned case for outsourcing solutions
    startups   exciting new   coming on-stream

    outside   the mob
    we need to engage   reach out
    the mob
    provide a new narrative
    speak to
    truth to power
    the mob

    exciting new startups   gone to tender
    your attendance is desired
    presentation   feedback   range of solutions
    accelerate change   key targets   change
    about managing expectations and impacts
    our bespoke streamlined solutions
    up your efficiency
    productivity issues
    interpersonal synergies
    reaching out

*

away from your duties   on secondment
providing auxiliary support
solutions for streamlining   key targets
everyone in   essential services cut back
it was exciting
managing change and expectations
impacts   exciting
no-one died
some went overnight   some went on gardening leave
but no-one actually died
it went over budget
and the roof fell in
a number of limbs stopped working
it was fine

*

but he just sits there
everyone else is doing their best but he just sits there
well there's nothing else to do apart from sitting   so you sit
you make the best of it though   or we do
he just sits there
and you feel that lack of respect
he can't be bothered with you as a person
but you keep on doing your best
you keep on talking
things to think about while you sit
or things you've thought about while sitting in the past
or things you haven't really thought about in detail yet while sitting,
but might like to, in the future, if you keep on having to sit
your dreams   ambitions   aspirations
having children   buying property
getting your kids the stuff the other kids have
and taking them abroad to play on a beach
the situation   all to do with it
the different ways of sitting
and the pressure points
the aches and pains
he just sits there
no respect

*

your hearing at Occupational Health
my name is Wilf   I lead this team   I'm pleased to meet you
benchmarked process   legal guidelines
case has been passed on to me
an obligation to comply
with centrally aggregated best practice
glad you've taken the opportunity to reach out with this issue
cascaded down
what you've applied for is no longer a certificate as such
unique identifier   captured
last year's process review uncovered a range of key strategic issues
opportunities for change
*your case is strong — in fact there are grounds for saying you meet the
key criteria already*
not a certificate now but a badge
new scheme   we're rolling out as of today
unique identifier   all good fun between colleagues
*early adopters are required to show a high-definition image, digitally
captured, of the exemptee's naked genitals and anus*
worn at all times in the presence of stakeholders
*incumbent on the exemptee to ensure that his or her anus is in a
reasonable state of cleanliness when the image of his or her anus is
presented for digital capture*
attached by means of a powerful magnet
in a state of non-arousal
survey data revealing that many respondents
objected to badges with pins
which damaged their clothing
full erections are prohibited
as are semi-erections, which evidence shows have been cultivated
tactically for the purposes of misleading colleagues, stakeholders and
accredited third parties regarding the size of a given adopter's sexual
organ in flaccidity*

uptake was high   retention was good
a slight majority of female over male adopters
approving the scheme
(would recommend to a friend)
visual traces of recent sexual emission are prohibited, as are emissions captured 'live'
they'd flagged you up as an early adopter
glans penis exposed   the prepuce retracted
Badge Scheme Champion
labia majora must be parted to expose the labia minora but not by more than fifteen millimetres or in such a way as to seek to arouse the viewer (if fingers are used, these should not be visible)
management keen to show   proactively
engagement with such intimate exposure
all-pervasive
not a top-down hierarchical imposition
but rather a synergized part of the institutional culture
senior management engaged
engaged proactively and passionately
there'd been focus groups   Away Days
cascading down   enhancing take-up
early adopters
Wilf pulled his trousers down   his pants
lay back on his desktop   spread his legs
retracted his foreskin
I myself am one of the Early Adoptment Champions
popped his phone down in front of his hairy perineum
to take a picture
could you squirt on some of that cleansing gel before I…?
it was a costly phone
his underwear, too, was expensive
logo   insignia   living the brand
you'll be aware by now   we pride ourselves
three-hundred-and-sixty-degree managerial practice

*

and it was actually, you know, the same for all of us
you couldn't move around
but he just sat there   while we others made the best of it
as best as we were able
making a joke to help keep it light
but he just sat there   like he thought he was above it all
the rest of us and how we'd chosen to deal with it
the sitting and having to sit
not that he said so   you just knew
he found the ways we tried to deal with it inadequate
no-one claimed it was ideal   no-one was under any illusions
keeping it light, and sharing your dreams and aspirations, having
children, buying property, getting your kids the stuff the other kids had
and taking them abroad to play on the beach, all that was part of
making the best of it
and generally the atmosphere was good   it was supportive
no-one was constantly in your face
but you could count on them if needed
despite the hormones flying about   the personality clashes
the spats and occasional bitchiness
you cared about each other
if you needed them
you knew
they'd be right there

*

you were in charge of him
achieving   he was determined
eyeball in close-up
expressive of terror

provide a new narrative
speak to
truth to power
the mob   outside   in charge
consultative process
something to steer by
nipple-shaped runestones cupped in a palm

he wasn't achieving
tubes and cannulas and tubes
despicable scrounger
pundits standing round   hushed voices
body enmeshed in its patchy chrysalis
popular vote
a protest   hands off
someone tripped the switch by accident
lights out

*

they had the right people in
but currently they were retraining
learning to reconnect   reach out
to colleagues and other key stakeholders
reaching out   going forward
wearing striped T-shirts a size too small for them
with cutaway nipple and navel features
cycling tights rolled up
to form a polo neck on each thigh
just staying relaxed now
cutaway crotch
if anyone needs to take a moment, that's perfectly fine
so no emergency fix for the lights
besides, your badge
or the roof fallen in
you haven't yet organized your badge?
old vulcanized bucket being a toilet behind a screen
perhaps your case worker
his case worker   Lucinda
might submit a formal request
the wobbling hire-bike   cutaway crotch
might get you further
try   submit

*

emergency measures
try the management   senior management
first/last venture down the corridor of power
there'd been focus groups   Away Days
full colour portraits
all too busy
brand ambassadors   wholly engaged
do not disturb
the juxtaposition on each office door
the face   the anus and the genitals
each office door
cascading down   enhancing take-up
of each occupant
no top-down hierarchical imposition
rather a synergized part of the institutional culture
lead by example

like they were chimpanzees
in a less-than-respectable zoo
engaged proactively
and passionately

*

the lights would come back on   but no time soon
strategic priorities
she was smiling   sympathetic
polite rejection seemed to be issuing from her vagina
and her anus was professionalism itself
he outlined clearly what the issues were
but his scrotum was doing the talking
you were bulldozed into the wall
his pendulous member   varicose
raggedy round the sleeve-end
probing the weaknesses of your argument
funk that choked you into submission
their open-door policy

*

not the restructuring to blame
there'd been a new one
nor the budgetary cuts
the impact of those swingeing cuts
on their business model   all to do with that
the budget had gone
they'd found a new one for the mob
the mob could believe them
now they were playing the game   coming clean
and it was amusing
breaking down silo mentalities
not pausing to reflect on what had been junked
as this would mean falling behind
and possibly being sprayed with liquid shit
new opportunities   exciting ones   elsewhere
no elsewhere left any more
you suspected

*

deep-cleaning solutions
maybe time call the contractors in
we're putting it out to tender
seal the area off
there's been a serious incident
we're implementing contingency plans
for outward-facing services and teams
we need to make it known
we've maintained continuity in accordance
with our published service standards
in the toilets
there's been an incident
a shittage
during the outage

*

what of the man
wrong end   a sewer pipe of shame
and soundless screaming
brick through the window

*

you wouldn't have minded
had no problem with the prospect of crawling through sewers
as long as they troubled to supply you
with the appropriate equipment
filter mask   full-body rubberized suit
perhaps an oxygen tank
a useful occupation
someone's got to
with abrasion-resistant gloves
an honest activity
you could fix things while you were down there
plug up some holes   unplug some blockages
it would be good
society needed people to crawl through sewers well
but when you looked into it they were too busy
strategic priorities
they were laminating their portraits
in accordance with their key strategic aims
revised going forward
as set out in the service catalogue
try   submit

*

frogmarched still
by else and back when
accused of a *disconnect*
perpetuating a disconnect
you hadn't earned your badge
disruptive influence   counter-collegiate
doing nothing   saying nothing
mindful felching
images beamed out live to the mob

*

the slurp of lubricant   the smear with
gossamer shock-victim foil of their capes
pinched round their shoulders as they knelt
the liturgy even better policed
their sperm-filled chalices
which the mob had provided
in readiness
taking more photos
plastic bowls between their legs
rebranded hire bikes
in each saddle embedded a camera
witness the closure and gape in the rising and falling
the going and coming
a must-see two or three seconds ago
now boring new key stakeholders to death

wind tussling and fussing around the breezeblocks
latest restructuring developments   scooping out
strategic   crenelated void
best not to dwell
the peer disapproval
scrambling   desperate to secure
determined   achieve
secure a place in the new regime
Lucinda   *rationalized existing structures for case work*
showed real leadership
competitive   more attractive to inward investment
Jim   *real leadership   managing clients' expectations*
measuring outcomes   I delivered on all the key outcomes
lined up   almost like a community
making the best of it
Ruby not so much a no-show   *gaining real traction*
under my leadership   across the piece

we hit and often exceeded   key performance targets
Maisie   welcome the chance to speak to this subject
one of the subjects I'm most   one of the many
most passionate
no-one was constantly in your face
but you could count on them if needed
Ronnie   put forward when my talent I guess was recognized
paid consultancy   obsession I have for granulizing key data
atmosphere good   it was supportive
Linnie   reaching out to colleagues across the piste
to firm up our networks   pipelines of synergy
never neglecting of course the need
and I think it's essential to have it
a healthy dose of fun
despite the hormones flying about
Wilf   three-hundred-and-sixty-degree assessment
hands-on role   enhancing take-up
understandable misapprehensions   coming on-stream
there's cause for optimism   I truly and firmly believe that
all we need   embrace a new narrative
personality clashes   new spats
despite all that   you knew if you needed them
they'd be there for you
they'd be there

*

brick through the window
tickling rivulet of faeces
natural wastage   what of the man
no longer staring
at a death that can't come soon enough
it can   it already has
no longer staring

reaching out
engaging strategically
the genius of the mob

*

had there been a disconnect
had human error crept in
they'd somehow left you out of the loop
you weren't invited to participate
in the latest strategic review
there wasn't a role for you
attendance neither compulsory nor desirable
gaps in the breezeblocks
cratered ledges   scurfy
metres over the threshold
grounds for optimism   new challenges
upward revision of your career path
how may I help you, sir
with compliments of the

have an outstanding weekend

www.ingramcontent.com/pod-product-compliance
Lightning Source LLC
Chambersburg PA
CBHW052136010526
44113CB00036B/2275